WHEN SOMEONE IN THE FAMILY DRINKS TOO MUCH

RICHARD C. LANGSEN   PICTURES BY NICOLE RUBEL

Dial Books for Young Readers New York

Published by Dial Books for Young Readers
A Division of Penguin Books USA Inc.
375 Hudson Street
New York, New York 10014

Text copyright © 1996 by Richard C. Langsen
Pictures copyright © 1996 by Nicole Rubel
All rights reserved
Designed by Amelia Lau Carling
Printed in Hong Kong
First Edition
1 3 5 7 9 10 8 6 4 2

Library of Congress Cataloging in Publication Data
Langsen, Richard C.
When someone in the family drinks too much /
by Richard C. Langsen;
pictures by Nicole Rubel.
p.   cm.
Summary: A self-help guide to enable children to
cope with alcoholism in the family setting.
ISBN 0-8037-1686-9 (tr.)—ISBN 0-8037-1687-7 (lib. bdg.)
1. Alcoholism—Juvenile literature. 2. Children of
alcoholics—Juvenile literature.
3. Alcoholics—Family relationships—Juvenile literature.
[1. Alcoholism.] I. Rubel, Nicole, ill. II. Title.
HV5066.L426 1996   362.29'23—dc20   94-39449   CIP   AC

The artwork for this book was created with black ink and colored markers.
It was then color-separated and reproduced in full color.

A note from the author

The children of alcoholic parents often feel responsible for the trouble they see in their family and don't understand that it is caused by a disease. They need to know that this disease called alcoholism is not their fault; alcoholics will continue to drink because they have an illness, not because someone has been "bad."

This book is meant to help such children feel less confused by what may be going on in their family and see that it is normal to have many conflicting feelings about an alcoholic parent or sibling—feelings of anger, hurt, and loneliness as well as love and anxiety. If children hint that there is some difficulty in their home, then most likely there really is a problem. We hope that this book will help young people who are troubled by such situations to talk about their feelings, to look at how they themselves have been behaving, and to encourage them to receive help. With help, children can learn to cope with this illness in a way that is healthy for them, and feel confident in their own inner strength.

What is an alcoholic?

An alcoholic is someone whose mind and body craves alcohol. Any drink, like beer or wine or whisky, that has alcohol in it makes an alcoholic ill.

Alcoholics have trouble controlling their drinking,

even when it hurts their family,

their job,

their health,

and their friends.

There are 28 million alcoholics in America.

One out of every ten people has this illness.

Most alcoholics are married or divorced,

most have jobs,

and many have children.

Alcoholics come from all walks of life.

They can be rich or poor.

They may be black, white, or brown.

They can be young or old,

and they might have had happy or unhappy childhoods.

Most experts agree that alcoholism hurts a person's mind and body.

There is no cure for it, but an alcoholic can stop getting sicker by not drinking alcohol anymore.

You might think this would be easy, but it really is a very hard thing to do.

Signs that someone may be an alcoholic

Although no two people are exactly alike, there are certain things that almost all alcoholics do. Someone you know may be an alcoholic if . . .

1 Drinking makes them not want to go to school, or to work.

2 They drink when they're alone, or they hide their drinking.

3 They forget things that happened while they were drinking. This kind of forgetting is called a *blackout*.

4 They seem mad or moody, or get angry easily when they've been drinking. Sometimes they lose control of themselves.

5 They pretend that they don't have a problem, or they get upset if you complain about their drinking. Sometimes they even lie about it.

6 They don't sleep well, they have accidents, and they are always tired when they've been drinking.

7 They would rather drink than go places or see friends.

8 They embarrass, harm, or worry their family and friends with their drinking.

9 They may promise to drink less and behave better, and they ask everyone to stop nagging them.

10 They drink alcohol frequently and in larger and larger amounts.

Confusing things that can happen

When someone in a family is sick with alcoholism, things that go on can be hard to understand.

Denial

Sometimes my mother pretends that she doesn't have this illness called alcoholism.

It's so weird: When I say Mommy is drinking too much, everyone tells me to keep quiet, or that I am wrong.

"Isn't Mommy drinking too much?"

"How dare you say that about your mother!"

Sometimes I play the game of denial too! I pretend everything is fine at home.

"Mommy can't come into work today. She has the flu."

Mood Swings

When my dad drinks, he acts differently.

Before my dad drinks, he is very helpful.

Model Space Shuttle

After he drinks, he becomes angry, and I am afraid of him. He's like two different people.

BEER

BEER

ER BEER BEER BEER

Blackouts

Sometimes when my mom drinks too much, she doesn't remember what she did.

Mom often doesn't remember what she did the night before. I get very confused when this happens.

I remember when my mom was drinking, I saw her wreck the car. The next day she didn't remember the accident.

Embarrassing Behavior

Sometimes I'm hurt or embarrassed by things my parents do when they drink.

One time my dad forgot to pick me up after a party at my friend's house.

Another time, when my friends came over to my house, my mom was asleep on the couch.

Once my dad and mom got into a fight with a policeman.

How a family is hurt by alcoholism

Enabler   **Perfect Child**   **Rebel**   **Lonely Child**   **Clown**

The alcoholic is not a bad person. He or she is a person with an illness who needs help to get well. However, when someone is sick with alcoholism, other family members may react in different ways.

The Enabler

When one person in a family has a drinking problem, a child or parent may try to make the problem go away, rather than dealing with it directly. This person is called the *enabler*.

The enabler tries to get the alcoholic to stop drinking.

The enabler thinks that hiding the alcohol may solve the problem.

The enabler may make excuses for the alcoholic, or do the chores for him or her.

Because drinking often makes the alcoholic feel sick, he or she does less and less, while the enabler takes over more and more of the family responsibilities and chores.

Sometimes enablers hide their feelings. Some people may deny that there is any problem at all, and others almost encourage an alcoholic to drink by always excusing his or her behavior.

Mom may be afraid to show Dad that she feels sad.

Sometimes she takes her sadness or anger out on a child instead of Dad.

She may be afraid that Dad will leave her if she shows how hurt she is.

He demands so much of her attention that she has little time for her children.

The Perfect Child

Older brothers and sisters often help the enabler. The "perfect" child gets attention by being very good and not causing trouble.

Perfect ones make the family look good. They think that if they are perfect, the alcoholic will become happy and not drink anymore.

At times the alcoholic rewards their perfect behavior, which makes them try to be even more perfect.

They usually act older than they are and don't allow themselves to act as goofy as other kids their age do.

They may feel ashamed of acting playful, making mistakes, or not being perfect.

What the perfect one feels inside:

Angry about having to work so hard.

Afraid of losing a parent's attention if they stop being perfect.

"I got an A plus on my math test."

Hurt when a parent or parents are critical.

"Where were you when I needed you?"

Sad at missing out on having fun with other kids.

The Rebel

The rebel gets attention by being bad.

If they can't get attention by being perfect, rebels get it by behaving badly.

Getting into trouble with friends will get rebels more attention from their parents.

Rebels can get Mom and Dad's attention by doing bad things at home.

The rebel is really angry with the alcoholic for drinking. And he or she is also angry with the enabler or the perfect child for the attention they give to the alcoholic, rather than to them.

Under the rebel's mask of anger are deeper feelings:

The Lonely Child

The lonely child doesn't try to be either perfect or bad. He or she just withdraws.

This child may find comfort in being alone.

He or she may have imaginary friends because it's too scary to have real ones.

"How are you today, baby bear?"

He or she watches too much TV, plays video games for hours, or just stays in his or her room and listens to music all day.

Lonely children may daydream when painful things are going on around them. Other people may not know that a lonely child feels bad. They just think the child likes being alone.

There is a lot of pain, though. A lonely child may think:

No one cares what I feel,

I have no friends,

I feel invisible,

I feel differently from everyone else.

The Clown

The clown learns that during the most painful moments, everyone in the family will stop fighting if the clown does something funny or acts cute.

Doing something funny can break up some very tense moments.

But by always clowning, clowns may forget to pay attention to important things, like their feelings or the feelings of those around them.

Friends may laugh at what a clown does, but after awhile they may think he or she is a nerd.

Sometimes clowns aren't taken seriously, when they really are in pain.

Underneath their joking are:

A strong need for attention,

a deep hunger for love,

a desire for approval,

and a fear that somehow they must ease the family tension or else things will get worse.

It's common to feel some of these ways when there is an alcoholic in the family

Afraid

Worried

Sad

Frustrated

Lonely

Confused

Upset

Guilty

Embarrassed

Hateful

Jealous

Ashamed

Shy

Bad

Sick

Not Noticed

Nervous

Awful

Hurt

Angry

Different

Things you can do to feel better

Remember that an alcoholic can get help and so can the whole family. Even if the alcoholic has stopped drinking and then starts again, do not be afraid. An alcoholic can get help again and be better again.

NEVER FORGET

You did not make the alcoholic sick. If one of your parents—or a brother or sister—is an alcoholic, he or she still loves you. The alcoholic may have a hard time showing love because alcoholism is an illness that prevents a person from behaving in a normal way.

You can . . .

Talk to someone you trust.

"Grandma, can we talk?"

Talk to sisters and brothers. Even though it might not seem like it, they are probably feeling some of the same things you are.

Learn about alcoholism.

Alcoholism

Alcohol and the Family

Tell yourself that IT'S NOT YOUR FAULT.

People and places
that may be able to help you

- Your family doctor, who can treat the physical problems of alcoholism and refer the alcoholic to a treatment program.

- Teachers and/or school counselors, who can provide information and help if you are having problems in school.

- Marriage and family therapists, social workers, psychologists, and psychiatrists, who can help you and your family cope and get better.

- The clergy and rabbis, who can be very helpful in guiding you to the right kind of help.

- Mental health centers. Many hospitals and state alcohol programs can give you information and counseling.

Some places that give free help

- The Phone Book. Look under Alcoholism, A.A., Al-Anon, or Narcotics Anonymous.

- Alcoholics Anonymous (also known as A.A.). This is a self-help program of recovering alcoholics. Throughout the world they have free meetings that try to help alcoholics.

- Al-Anon. These groups have free meetings that are just for the families and friends of the alcoholic. Al-Anon teaches people how to live or cope with someone who is an alcoholic.

- Alateen. This is the same as Al-Anon except that it is for young people from ages 12 to 20 who have an alcoholic friend or family member.

- Al-A-Tot. This is like Al-Anon and Alateen but is for children under 12.

- Adult Children of Alcoholics (ACOA). This is a free group that helps people who grew up in an alcoholic family.